Transplanted

Terry Ann Carter

D1598234

Canada

*The Publishers acknowledge the financial assistance of the
Government of Canada through the Book Publishing Industry Development Program
(BPIDP) for our publishing activities.*

Library and Archives Canada Cataloguing in Publication

Carter, Terry Ann, 1946-
    Transplanted / Terry Ann Carter.

Poems.
ISBN 0-88887-311-5

    1. Life change events—Poetry. I. Title.

PS8555.A77296T73 2006   C811'.54   C2006-901115-X

Cover collage by Claudia Radmore
Cover image used with permission from Radiology Centennial, Inc.
Author's photo: Len Douglas
Printed and bound in Canada on acid free paper.

Transplanted

Terry Ann Carter

Borealis Press
Ottawa, Canada
2006

for Darryl, who gave me this book,
and for Dylan and Barrett

I chose poetry because every line set out
so hopefully from a new margin, and
because my heart was hot and unbowed.

Michele Leggott

Contents

Post-Op

Pre-Op

Prognosis

Just before suppertime
in a two room laboratory,
Professor Wilhelm Roentgen
discovers X-rays, a shimmer turning
to green florescence.

With a pear-shaped glass container
and cyanide painted on a screen,
he offers a bold hypothesis.

Weeks later, the tannenbaum trimmed
in an upstairs parlour, he bombards
the bones of his wife's left hand,
fifteen minutes to burn an image of fingers,
skinless knuckles,

the opaque wedding ring.
Some objects more easily passed into —
some marriages shocked by light.

Plain Song

God is a technician reading X-ray charts
a mouth shaping words.

An airline pilot
with the voice of a radio announcer

advising us by cell phone not to worry.
The ambulance driver

waiting by the side of the road.
This is thin ice, getting thinner

the blue flame of a match
just struck.

We take it all
on trust.

Star Attraction

Before your transplant, I begin
to dream about them: kidney beans,
kidney shaped pools.
Pool ques poke kidneys
instead of billiards.
They fly in V-formations.

Kidneys in the faces of flowers, lurking
beneath the back deck.
Blubbery interviews
on prime time radio.

Driving home over back roads,
I almost hit a ground hog, slam
on my brakes to watch it waddle off
to the woods
like a fat, fuzzy kidney.

And on sleepless nights, TV kidneys
swivel their hips, sing back up
for Gladys Knight

ain't nothin like the real thing, baby

The Skin of Cantaloupe

It can distract me for a whole morning,
with stories: Aunt Shirley falling in love
in Texas, with a field of cantaloupe.
mounds of heaven
she used to say, bending down
hands gloved against snakes,
to cut their stems, gathering
them to her bosom.

Our first apartment.
You climbing the stairs
two at a time, hippie hair
bouncing on your shoulders.
Taxi tales to last for hours.
Hey babe, here's one you'll like –

driving the girls home
from their strip club joints,
late night trips across the river.

Luscious, pale fruit
beneath the skin of cantaloupe,
exotic breasts jiggling in the back seat
of your cab. The secrets
you must have kept.

Night Train

A knock at our door, passports checked
one more time. Before babies we travel
to Prague by night train, leave
the German border in a cluster of tidy lights.

You fall asleep; I make my way
to the dining car where white linen cloths
sway under candlelight, steady
my steps like Ingrid Bergman
entering Rick's café.

Without a broad brimmed hat
and lace stockings, the scene's wasted;
yet I think of her, the arched eyebrows.

Out of my window the tiniest of moons,
a couple at the next table whisper
in words I do not understand.
A reflection of trees floats against glass,
Bergman's eyes brim.

It is better not to know
what follows.

Prague Suite

1.
Across this dark distance
of dimly lit statues, clouds
pass over the sombre towers of churches.
I lean against the Charles Bridge
hands resting on old stones,
gaze into evening water.
These saints protect us
from X -ray reports, hospital
corridors, and I think of you, Kafka,
your sad phrases with me now
just below my tongue.

2.
In Malostrenske Square
the string quintet, assembles
for Dvorak's dances. An old man
tucks his viola under his chin,
dreams of paradise
in the new world order.
.

3.
The sun tries to warm
our brittle bones, we walk
in rain to a small café, a quiet place
to stir coffee and speak of strategies.
Under a grey sky
that frowns and offers
only fallen leaves, we suspend
our fears, forget the climb of creatinine.

Later, we will choose a restaurant
advertised in the hotel brochure,
a gentleman will escort us
to our table. There will be
candles and a litany of wines.
Oh! the prospect
of strawberry soup.

Diagnosis

Bedtime stories for our two
young sons, skin against skin,

our evenings folded
in origami of the flesh,

not yet aware of
how an X-ray will change

the way sleet falls, ice
glittering black

on innocent stretches
of highway.

Gardener 1: Moths Rising

Just the edge of shadow
against a plate of glass
is enough to prepare the heart
for survival, an X-ray's ability
to change the shape
of things to come.

Driving up the lane way
the car brushes against mounds
of amethyst sage, triggers
a cloud of tiny, yellow wings.
Sulphur moths hidden in the lattice
of leaves and underbrush
swell the air, explode upward,
outward.

Again, technicians translate
coded messages within
the design of X-rays, the shadows
on your kidneys framed by light.

And for this moment
I see them again,
rising from sage
at dusk.

Light Matter

The body rejects
what it does not know:
cesium, plutonium –
the aftermath of Hiroshima, Nagasaki,
Chernobyl's strontium tricking cells.
The immune system ruined,
a chaos of complication.

And yet,
these folds of light, life-giving –
the first form of it, translated
from Genesis, the fires of caves
and cave dwellers, torches to blaze
ancient citadels. Japanese maples
alight in late afternoon. Amber
from the Baltic coast, electric
in a crescent shaped pin.

The invention of bulbs, halogen,
laser, Christmas lights twinkling
over the women's shelter,
my grandmother's pilot light.
The shine of a street lamp, alarm clock,
dash board. The headlights of your Chevy
as we drove into the blizzard.

Nothing in his childhood
prepared Wilhelm Roentgen
for the arrival of rays. Perhaps he watched
birds, or scribbled notes in a wire bound notebook —
never knowing the glow from his laboratory
would light the future.

Or Marie Curie, in Paris,
uncovering a luminosity, a gift
for her husband – radium, a weapon
in the hands of oncologists.

X-rays, these matters of light
a hurly-burly vibration
or the meditation of monks,
how we move through our days
a flapping of wings, sudden,
in the silent fields.

Adolescence

Did Roentgen, the teenager, dream of girls?
never daring to speak, turning to science –

physics providing laws
for substances he could touch.

At a masked ball, disguising himself
as the archangel

falling out of heaven
on the head of a pin

his serious mindfulness
falling out of fashion

with the ladies of Wurzburg.
Never claiming a prize

for best dressed —
never claiming a prize for wit.

Roentgen did, however, go on to win the Nobel Prize for Physics in 1901.

Florentia Bella

While you wait to see the nephrologist
I disappear into the travel poster
on the wall, resurrect Giotto's city,
Dante's, too, Brunelleshi's Duomo
behind glass, the journey's end
for pilgrims. Outside, I'm sure, the air
is scented with lemons, olives
sweet oranges, figs. Fancy takes me
to the chapel Michaelangelo built
for the Medici, orchard, palazzo,
thousands of flowering trees.
This is good, good, but it can't
last, is bringing me to the corner
where I scribbled a postcard, close
to the spot where Savonarola burned.

Gardener 2: Divinity

I am learning to diagnose
the ailments of plants,
bits of blight, leaves
curling under with ticks.

I begin early. Plant
young seedlings in Styrofoam cups
spread out on the piano seat
in southern exposure.
A few will survive.

Such holiness in this scooping:
planting, watering, waiting.
My arms rise in benediction;
the green leaves, grow.

Glued to Ice

The hockey moms gather
in early morning arenas, hands
wrapped around hot mugs
of coffee, eyes still bleary
from sleep. One of the women,
a cardiac nurse, fills
us in on coronary politics
stories of mis-diagnoses.

Another mom, a pharmacist,
forecasts new allergy meds,
the brands to stay away from.
Again, our eyes wide with disbelief.
How can it be? someone asks.

We are concerned about
the slashing and body checking
up and down the ice. What is it
exactly our boys are learning?

I watch my son take a penalty
for raising his stick to a bully.
The crowd thumps feet on the cold
cement floor, players shake sticks
against air.

He skates off to the "sin bin",
the mothers continue to listen
to prognoses. I try not to think
of the coming operation, discard
the hospital gossip. I keep
my eyes glued to the ice,
my ears to the spin of skates.

Someone's son scores.
We are on our feet,
voices triumphant
over the loudspeaker.

Honey, Let's Take A Holiday

Canadian winters, so cold,
snow flakes falling like
two dollar coins. I'm stuck
in Queensway traffic, sleet
between my windshield wipers,
blues on the radio. It's time to
get away, perhaps Marina Casino
in Key West. We've been there before.

Key West, where the festival
for its favourite son, unleashes
a flurry of look-a-likes, prompts
discussions on post modernism.
We're all trying to remember
a Hemingway quote, but
by three o'clock, everyone's
at the beach drinking cola and rum.

By evening, a rooftop restaurant.
White lights strung through trees.
Someone's playing Bill Evans
at the piano bar, we dig into
Papa's dolphin fish.

Shades of night roll in
like whitecaps.

Ridge

Out for a walk
this silvered night,
my breath a frosty ring.
Snow sticks to the bottom
of my boots, and the trees'
black boughs stretch
into the sky. It is a
brief distraction.

I climb the hill
to Bruce Pit, where shards of ice
crumple near stone,
and the moon casts
a milky white spell.

Earlier today, I misjudged
a student, saw in his eyes
the reproach from yet, another
adult, heard the locker door slam —

still

up here on this ridge
amid spruce and pine,
the snow offers
quiet absolution.

Standing In Front of Statues

We're clustered on palace steps
on a good day. Beaming
into the camera lens,
this is an afternoon to be framed.

Five years before your transplant
the family travels to Salzberg,
home to Mozart, the River of Salt.
A performance of Magic Flute —
and we watch Papageno in mottled feathers
rustle against his cage of fear

like the four of us imprisoned in film
our innocent eyes unable to look away.

Fish Poem for Barrett

My son walks his fish home
in a plastic bag next to his skin,
his belly rounded with a new kind of flesh,
the glassy road a mirror beneath his feet.

In the house, he unzips his jacket —
fingers slow and cranberry red.
He removes the watery shell
from his warm body, examines
the fish in the light.

When he sleeps
the light is switched off.
He tells me the fish are dreaming,
perhaps, of high stone walls
fins outstretched like the wings of planes
or hurtling through grassy fields.

In the morning he rubs his eyes,
peers through near-sightedness.
Tracing fingers against cool glass,
he waits for fish kisses.

Grey

My car comes to a stop
between the yellow painted lines
and before the engine dies,
the undeniable notes of the opening
to Albinoni, the cello rising over
asphalt and red shopping carts.

A crumpled newspaper rolls
like a tumbleweed
from an old Western.

In the side mirror
a flutter of gulls, circling
a single light standard.
Hundreds of wings
in the darkness of air,
and I am weeping
in the parking lot
of the I.G.A.

Dreaming Mexico

1.
It is easy to slip into this reverie
pull on the skin of death and faith –
a place where Frida and Diego
danced with alebrijas, fifteen foot high
papier mache beings, created
for the Day of the Dead.

A two week haven where I searched
for Posada's prints, the fashionable Calavera
in a Sunday hat. Toy skeletons popping up
in children's books, glazed
on the tops of cookies, cakes.

Everywhere, the rattle of bones
and voices, pushing me into shrines
for Our Lady of Gaudeloupe,
shouting at me to *wake up,*
pay attention, daring me
to pray.

2.
I love being a woman, brushing
my hair, seated on a rooftop
on Umaran Street, the long strokes
arcing my arm like a crescent moon.
I love the bristles
catching in my palm,
the stray strands gathered
left to float on the wind
like some docile dragonfly.

From here I can view
avocado, mango trees
pigeons in clusters over cobblestones.
I can feel the afternoon
turning to dusk, ochre
fleeing to moss green,
the silvery pale of laurel leaves
twisting through iron gates.
I can taste the bright
radish coloured cactus fruit.

I love being a woman, lifting
my arm to brush my hair, brushing
my hair on Umaran Street.

Forbearance

In English class, we read
a poem by Henry David Thoreau,
marvel at his detail for nature,
his civil disobedience.
We try a passage from Melville,
I tell them he always
dreamed of the sea.

Who knew that I would need
such forbearance, a word
from my New England past
a place for pioneers
and independence.

Trapped here, in this classroom,
adolescence grafted onto these editions
like fingerprints that never lose their touch.
My arms reach for Emily Dickinson
and the love she left, unopened,
in her bottom bureau drawer.

Grammar Lesson

We start at the beginning of your paragraph.
I point out that you are loving
in the present tense
and that syntax
does not allow
for having been loved
in the past —

that we write in the same tense
within a given space
and what I really mean to say
is that
it is important to have been loved
and to go on loving
even though a modern alphabet
unlocks a language
of doubt.

poems

what I always remembered
about the dead boy
was
the day
he offered
two poems
folded
inside a shell

the way
he
placed them
on my desk
turning on his heel
to leave
the room

Flute Music for Camille

On an altar quiet with blossoms,
 her young death reminds of us of heaven.
I watch my students in their grief
suspended without buoyancy.
They hug each other
in disbelief.

The silver flute
rolls in to my mouth
I pause for steady breathing.
The Bach prelude.
Notes rise.

There is something here
that saves us
gives us bone
beneath the skin.

These Things That Vanish

Afternoon invites us to wander
through other peoples' lives.
Here, in the antique shop, with silver
tea strainers and dresser scarves
tatted in lace, an old fashioned
wicker of love.

As a girl, I weighed the hours, waited
on the porch for my father's return
from work. He would walk up the path,
past birdhouse and fountain, the glowing
pink of magnolia blossoms, lift me
high into sunlight.

Once, in winter,
I waited past dinner,
past the sting of redness in my cheeks
the dull bone chill of December.
And then he appeared, designs
for fantastical creatures
rolled up under his arm.

We fashioned them there,
on the front lawn, two mythical beasts,
with swaying backs and little mounds
of snow decorating their manes.
Lions' legs like Ozymandias'
stretching across four corners,
and a tail that curved
behind the left flank. We were astride
fleeing the imaginary jungle
our laughter ringing like temple bells
over white. A father and his eldest daughter
in darkness
in the holy work of play.

In the antique shop
my hands rest on the burled wood
of beds; I imagine bridal wreaths
and white rhododendron.
These things that vanish sadden me:
snow lions
melting in sun.

Gardener 3: The Quilted Heart

In a television documentary
on poetry and nature
a woman tries to convince me
that the heart is a quilted thing,
its blood drawn through
a net of solaced roots,
an applique of lime and humus.
It is a plant in need of repair.

Morning, she says,
may be embroidered with paths
through stones and leaves
through dried sticks
from the farmer's field
each groove, an impression
of natural light
stitching the earth with roses
and honeysuckle,
the vining of petals and bloodroot.

The only blood I know
is measured in vials,
pinpricks in the arm
that later turn blue,
muscles hardening
after too many times
and the arm too sore
to move.

Blood
tested for similarities
so that a sibling might show
where love is kept,
a thread of vein
hemming the edges
of leaves.

Fuli Wah's on Somerset Street

After a morning's hospital visit
we find ourselves on the second floor

of our favourite Chinese restaurant.
In the early days we order

sticky rice rolled in lotus leaves
chicken moo goo guy pan and

chow mein some foo youngs
chop sueys and szechuan shrimp

the names of our selections
little poems wrapped in sauces.

Later, you will not be able to eat —
content enough to savour

the sights and smells
the blessed event of the ordinary.

Dylan's Sky

Midnight comes.
My older son is calling
from a cell phone
stopped by the side of the road.

Look outside, Mom.
Go to the driveway
and look up.

I am standing
at the edge of the garden
near the blighted oak,
gathering a sweater
around my shoulders.

I see it.
Slight rumblings,
undulations of fault lines
sweeping heaven, small
explosions of arterial light.

Standing for minutes
my neck arched and straining,
my body begins to tremble
with the joy of it.
This northern light, like petals,
dropping around me.

Red

Miranda welcomes us to her workshop.
We begin our warm-ups

like butterflies charging jacaranda bushes.
Our legs swinging, flesh tucked

beneath the bony ridge. She explains
chakra, the significance of colour,

how the strong delicate shell
of body rises like music

our shoulders arched
in warmth, in waves.

Here we breathe out of crimson lips
feel love against our skin.

Bluebonnets

My sister's laughter is the track
I travel down, meeting
in this mid-Texas town
our hearts crisscrossed with history.
Daddy taught school here
kept horses
drove a hay truck.

In this part of the South
young boys bend on one knee
in front of knotted trees, learn
to distance themselves
from the click of a trigger
and a bull's eye shot, close
one eye, aim and fire
never missing a blink
never missing the P
in a Dr. Pepper can.

We climb a sandy road
to the large white house
past pecan trees, mesquite,
the clutch of a devil's claw.
Armadillo shells lie scattered
bone bleached like an O'Keefe painting.

Suddenly, a patch of blubonnets
and we stop to gather the day
in our arms, these wild and spikey blooms
soon, to disappear.

Sometimes, It Surrounds Us

In those early days, on vacation
with the children, winding our way
through country roads, stopping
at the Falls in Niagara
the deer farm close by

you took a photograph
of me on my knees –
three fawns close to my arms
our boys just out of reach.

Perhaps, that day
I began my prayers
in the off-hand way
that mothers do,
surrendering to that pure light.

Celebrating V-E Day at the Legion

Fifty years later, we roast hot dogs
at the community legion, listen to swing—
our hips not able to move in the same
easy manner as our mothers' once did.

Our mothers who know this music
instantly, hum whole bars long after
the song is gone, our mothers who rode
the A Train, The Chattanooga Choo Choo

who bought bonds, darned socks,
jitterbugged the lobby of the Plaza Hotel.

Fifty years later, at this picnic table,
we raise glasses in an odd salute
try to imagine what it once was like,
our eyes closed in the dark.

Later in bed, we do not speak
of mothers, or your illness,
not even the nightly news
and weather. Breathing in unison
we lie side by side, shrouded in silence.

Before Deciding On Transplant

My brothers drive motorcycles
my son, too,
their hard arms leaning
across metal, helmets tight to their heads.

Today in traffic
I pass an accident,
a Harley in a heap
by the side of the road.

All the articles
I've been reading
imply a perfection
in these victims, excellent
donors, brain damaged
while other parts stay intact.

We have been told
the cadaver kidney
can be carried in a Pepsi cooler
rushed by taxi
to the operating room.

Those flailing limbs
one last gesture of benediction —
the fine line that might divide
your solace,
from someone else's suffering.

Needing Butterflies

1.
After the body's pulse
causes the flush of fever,
the stomach retching up itself
until only strands of green mucus
leave their trails down the stainless steel sink—
there is a need for butterflies,
to watch them tremble
against the greenhouse wall,
afternoon rain leaking
through the roof.

2.
Flowers that attract lepidoptera:
ageratum, alyssum, daylily
are among others
whose scent seduces.

Such nectar
on a sunny day
and shelter from the wind.

3.
Muscles in the thorax
force the fulcrum of flight

a slanted figure eight
propels the moth

like an airplane.
A thin layer

protects the body
thousands of tiny scales

lending colour and light,
wings strengthened by veins.

4.
In a book about Japanese poetry
I read about moth imagery,
the opening and closing of wings
a symbol for erotic love,
arousal superior
to the act itself.

This explains the tradition
of watering down stones
placed in a garden
to greet a lover, a premonition
of light and air and touch.

5.
At three a.m., moths quiver
around the front porch light,
my teenaged sons still out.

Unable to sleep, I roam the house
counting tiles over the kitchen sink,
wooden boards in the floor.

My shoulders not able to relax
until I hear the turning of a key,
their footsteps down the hall.

6.
They called her the butterfly queen
the girl who sat behind me in history
the first girl to have sex
in our grade twelve class.
She did IT, they all said
referring to her boyfriend
as a pig, never knowing
that she secretly enjoyed the teasing.
TBQ was a nickname
established after her homecoming
stint, the wings of a giant costume
purchased by the PTA.
With white go-go boots
and beehive hairdo
she was the envy of us all.

At our 25th reunion
we learned she was killed
in an accident, driving home
on a summer's night, her two young babies
thrown from their seats.
Our eyes fluttering,
folding in tears.

Gardener 4: Without Marigolds

Once, working in her garden,
she told me
she would probably
never have children —
never co-create a life.

How could she have known
that years later
she would have this sisterly
chance to perform a miracle,
a correct combination
of blood type and t-cells
the ultimate gift
one doctor said.

In a fairytale film made in India
she would be the princess
carried through streets, orange marigolds
tossed into air. Drapery silks woven
with mauve, tangerine, sky blue.
Three trained elephants would bow
at her feet as the maharajah
raised her hand to his lips.

But this is ordinary time
on an ordinary street
where she walks to work
each day, listens to her
favourite radio station.

An ordinary day
when all the credits have slipped
from view, the music, too,
dimmed into darkness,
all the actors removing make-up
sitting with scripts in hand,

figuring out the roles
to play, the plants to cherish
and maintain
in the cosmic garden.

Tonight, her hand rises
to close the blind, shuts out
the fear of moonlight. Her gift
will be given tomorrow,
without marigolds.

Transplanted

1.
How can we prepare
for this new script,
a plot constructed
from certain chromosomes
askew in your body.

An introduction to characters
complete with crisis, denouement.

Dialogue with doctors who never
tell us everything
we need to know,
figuring it out alone
a Rubik's cube too large
for any fingers.

2.
Nothing I could say
would change the way you feel

my hands in the air
with questions

Can I get you some hot soup?
Would you like a tea   ... with lemon?

Sometimes, I can't finish a sentence
your answer pouring over me

no, no there's not
a goddamned thing you can do!

3.
Kidney disease fills the house,
dominates our conversations.
With one son getting ready
to leave home, the other one
nestling in, their lives a constant
plunge into adolescent pools.
Their rooms, retreats —
floor-to-ceiling archives.
My day job pounding
on the front door, somewhere
an alarm clock ringing.

Some days I love you.
Who did you think you married
anyway, Florence Nightingale?

4.
The night covers us
with something more
than just a search for fingers
to hold on to. In a dream,
a leopard sniffs by the back door,
senses the surgeon's scalpel.
Words tendril out, shoot skyward.
Eyes and implements glitter.

John Wayne and the Beaches of Normandy

The hospital provides a social
worker, for partners of the ill.
Someone who listens, carefully.

My first appointment
and her energy draining me —
so bouncy, so much fun
wound up like a talking doll.

Later, a Brit
who races motorcycles,
his Harley parked in the laneway.
He is patient, consoling
and male,
what would he know?

Third, the grey-haired earth mother,
who fills my sessions with reports
of her own illness, charting
unknown territory,
the ups and downs
of changing blood tests,
her own metaphorical
transplant.

Some days
all I think of
is the differences between us,
the ways we choose to heal.
You with your war movies
and sex-is-a-solution to everything
and me, closing our door
for days on end
not letting in, even, the light.

Night Before Surgery

Such a distrust I carry
for places like these –
hospitals with antiseptic smells,
nurses who ask for
"Christmas presents"

where doctors promised
my mother, my father would be home
in a week or two. Like a Boy Scout,
you have packed a small bag.

I walk with you
past the nurses' station
where they all seem to be laughing
over someone's joke, or perhaps
it's gossip. Who can tell?

Outside, the sun is setting.
The sky turns pale yellow
behind the blackened branches.

Origami

Skin can be cut,
shaped into layers, with corners
touching corners, skillfully manipulated
through blood, tendon, muscle, fat.

In a transplant, an organ
passed from one body
to another, is an allegory
of this cherry petal season

when rhododendrons sparkle
and sunlight bounces off
your blue eyes. A surgeon
conceives a new shape.

Hands scrubbed, ready,
he begins the first cut.
Already the artifact
takes form.

> *It is worth remembering*
> *Sadako, the Hiroshima girl*
> *and her thousand cranes,*
> *her folding.*

On this April morning
in a light downpour
of pollen and daffodils,
flesh makes way for flesh:
your sister's kidney
no larger than a fist
light as a bird.

Post-Op

Peeling My Grandmother's Potatoes

Knife's first cut, and I can smell
the bogs of County Clare, see
my grandmother's tongue clenched
between her teeth,
her blue veined fingers twisting
the brown peels of her potatoes
around the litany of saints,
the mysteries of her *most holy rosary*
that she prayed every night
of my childhood.
Standing at the kitchen sink
she began the *glory be's*, spreading her belief
like a warm cloth over bread, her religion
regular as the seasons.

My grandmother never questioned.
Stood her place in the House that shielded
her from anguish and torment,
always seemed to know what to do.

God looks after those
who look after themselves.

In a waiting room during your surgery
I pray for my grandmother's faith,
wanting it to be a hard, white, orb —
solid, in my palm.

Elemental

After surgery, I visit
in i.c.u., hands and body
covered so germs
will not intrude.

You lie peacefully,
your chest's rhythm the only
familiar. The strange tangle
of monitors and tubes.

The doctors say
your production of urine
the following day,
even three drops of gold
will ensure success,
fight the scourge
of an early rejection.

Sunset over Key West.
Mallory Square.
The last golden beam
sizzling
down
into
the
sea.

Pavane

Even the cat
is missing you, rubbing
her back against
your chair.

The house settles
into its night noises —
furnace, fridge, wooden floor.

Outside a moth
circles the porch light.
The sky is black
and starless.

First Visitor

Catheter attached to a long pole,
you begin to walk down corridors.
Intravenous dangles from your arm.

In the hospital sunroom
your first visitor, a photographer
friend, offers dope under the folds
of your gown. He is already flirting
with the floor nurse.

Knowing your passion for cars
he keeps you on track
with the eternal debate:
BMW vs. Benz, picks up speed
with talk of engines, gossip
from the Monaco Grand prix,
his prize winning shots of Gilles
Villeneuve, the pit stop
scoops. He asks if you have your
eye on a new one
(sports car, that is)

Abso - bloody - lutely
you answer.

The revved up talk
has taken its toll, afternoon light
hurts your eyes. You begin the slow walk
back to your room. Wind,
already in your hair.

White

How do simple things
get so complicated?
(Have I told you, today,
I love you?)

Opals,
moonflowers,
milk in the pitcher,
all these pleasures
do not compare
to that calm white on white
snow light —
the loneliness of moonlight,
when you are not here.

Premiere

Nights pass in a wilderness
of waking,
it has been eleven days
since your transplant.

I am at the symphony, alone,
the seat beside me haunted
by your shape, the fold of shirt
over your chest, your body's quiet breath.

In the liner notes I read
"the night is shattered
and the blue stars shiver in the distance"
a line from Neruda to inspire
sleigh bells, water gongs,
bowed vibraphones creating
a mystical heaven.

Such solace
in these shimmering cymbals
and flutterings of alto flute,
as if heart beats emerge
from the spaces between
temple bells – steady undeniable
droplets of sound, pulsing
like a bedside monitor.

Recovery

Still
in April
you need a blanket
covering your knees.
You sit
on the back deck
facing the sun.

For a moment
you look
like a passenger
on some elegant
ocean-going vessel
your eyes
focusing
on the horizon.

The Women Arrive

With baskets of fruit,
Easter eggs,
bracelets, earrings jangling,
they use all the right words
flowing into air
filled with scent
of honeysuckle, freesia, musk.

They are on the back deck
pouring tea into china cups,
slicing cheese to serve
on bread, crackers.
The little olives in a row.

The women have arrived
with solace, comfort,
wrapped in fuchsia tissue,
poking out of gift bags. They
offer blessings with arms curved
and outstretched.

Botticelli and the Secrets of Married Life

The wasp in a detail of *Venus and Mars*
is a play on images, the work commissioned
by Vespucci, (Italian for wasp).
In a lecture at the museum
countless secrets, guarded by canvas -
the name of Renoir's daughter's
piano teacher, embossed
on the edge of sheet music.

After thirty years of marriage
it is important to remember
the gifts we have given each other:
the heart shaped spoons you purchased
in Italy, in the silver shop near the Spanish Steps.
The photograph I gave you
of a Taiwanese kite master,
an amorous note, coded
in Chinese calligraphy, floating
in clouds over the South China Sea.

Transfusion

Galleries are silent places
where lovers hold hands, gaze
into artwork, luminous as their eyes.

Here is Kahlo's yellow, vermillion,
her crucified nails biting
into blood. We discuss it all –
the wherefore's, the why's.
What makes a good painting, anyway?
Can art be too personal, closing its doors
on innocent eyes, afraid to look any closer.

We decide it's the creation
that's important. Using a brush
to leave a space, colour to let us breathe.

This museum, a summer garden,
a shelter for me and the lion haired woman
who keeps me company.
Our talk, an amber medicine.

Leitmotif: or, A Short History of Renal Transplant

Total body X-ray.
Marrow infusion, survival
a crap shoot. Three years after WWII,
an artificial organ emerges.

Red and white cells
a semaphore for survival, allographs
for identical twins. All of this
came before.

You never knew
the lists of drugs, experiments
with rabbits, mice. Your sister's kidney
placed into your lower abdomen,
the way we lowered baby Jesus
into the crèche, bits of straw
sticking every which way.

Birthday

The first snow
since your transplant
your life is still measured
by tests: blood, urine —
trips to the clinic,
the number of days
since we knew
that this was to be
our future,

and today
your birthday. We tease you
about your feminine implant
your new sensitive side,
all of us, giddy
with renewal.

Later, when the family leaves,
I walk with you down the driveway,
remember your first, five, steps
in the hospital ward.
Your stubborn, male, determination.

Transparencies

Uncertain of his creation,
Wilhelm Roentgen uses X,
the mathematical unknown,
to name his rays.

Theatres, at the time, produce
X-ray plays, characters on stage
with wizard-like beards. Cartoons
in newspapers feature crystal balls.
Could X-ray eyes foresee the future?

This association with spirits,
images of skeleta frightening.
Such an interest
in the invisibility of things.
Paper, wood, aluminum
becoming transparent.

In marriage, the disappearance
of self, our bodies shimmering
into darkness. How we strive
to shape our own bones.

That White Blur, Astounding

Desire, also, atrophies
like the kidneys left
inside you
to wither, dissolve —
particles moving, entering
the bloodstream.

At midlife I am aware
of my body's lapses,
how the mind takes
subtle vacations
over mountainous terrain
or a nostalgia tour
through childhood,
how brief messages
left on the phone
or e-mail, catapult
me into another dimension.

This is just one more
obstacle to overcome.
Given time, or so the specialists
tell us, desire's flame
will emerge once more,
that white blur, astounding
us both.

X-ray Love

On Valentine's Day
you placed your hands
on the small bones
between
my breasts.

Acknowledgements

Some of these poems have appeared (in earlier forms) in the following journals: *Arc, Vallum, Dandelion, Grey Borders, Heritage, Museletter* (League of Canadian Poets), *Carleton Arts Review, Bywords*

"These Things That Vanish" and "Celebrating V-E Day at the Legion" appear in *Soundings*, Buschek Books, 2005

"Peeling My Grandmother's Potatoes" was a finalist in the Canadian Authors Association Poetry Contest, 2004

"Star Attraction" appeared in Body Language: A Head to Toe Anthology, Black Moss Press, 2003

"Forbearance" was a finalist in the National League of American Pen Women - Palomar Branch, 2002

"Prague Suite" and "The Gardener 3: The Quilted Heart" were finalists in the Ray Burrell Award for Poetry, 2000

"Fish Poem for Barrett" and "Bluebonnets" appeared in *Anapanasati*, a chapbook, published by Cranberry Tree Press, 1999

"Skin of Cantaloupe" appeared in *Tender Journeys/Thirteen Ottawa Women Writers*, (edited by Candis Graham) 1999

Thank you to the Ottawa Poetry Group where some of these poems were first workshopped, particularly, Ronnie R. Brown, for indefatigable support, encouragement and friendship; and to Baggio's Poetry for Thursday night sessions and good Italian food

Thank you to the Feminist Caucus of The League of Canadian Poets for inspiration and support

Thank you to Sue McMaster for teaching me to ask questions, to Gary Geddes for his time and patience and sense of humour, and to Monty Reid for a final read under the dinosaurs

Thanks also to Russell E. Smith, Holly Kritch, and Dina Cox

in memoriam, "past the stars" Marianne Bluger and Candis Graham

Thank you to friends and colleagues at Mother Teresa High School, St. Joseph High School, Gloucester High School, and D. Aubrey Moodie Middle School where I have appeared as Poet-In-The-School. And to the "glory days" of the English Department at St. Paul High School where it all began.

Dedications

"Origami" is for Dr. P. Barron, The Ottawa Hospital.

"Florentia Bella" is for Dr. G. Posen, The Ottawa Hospital.

"Premiere" is for Alexina Louie whose composition "Dark Nights Shivered Stars" premiered with the National Arts Centre Orchestra, April 16, 1997.

"Bluebonnets" is for my sister, Marianne Hamilton.

"Forbearance" is for Ronnie R. Brown, another transplanted New Englander.

"The Women Arrive" is for the YaYa's.

"Honey, Let's Take a Holiday" is for Billy Hawkins.

"poems" is in memory of Cameron Lozinski.

"Transfusion" is for Claudia Coutu Radmore.

"Gardener 1: Moths Rising" is for Adele T. Aquino.

"Gardener 2: Divinity" is for Philomene Kocher.

"Gardener 4: Without Marigolds" is for my sister-in-law, Janet Carter.

MEMBER OF SCABRINI GROUP

Québec, Canada
2006